The Rough Drafter

A Guide to Rough Drafting
for the Indie Author

RSK

HYPER NOSTALGIA

Contents

"In the darkness something was happening at last. A voice had begun to sing. It was very far away and Digory found it hard to decide from what direction it was coming. Sometimes it seemed to come from all directions at once. Sometimes he almost thought it was coming out of the earth beneath them. Its lower notes were deep enough to be the voice of the earth herself. There were no words. It was hardly a tune. But it was beyond comparison, the most beautiful sound he had ever heard. It was so beautiful he could hardly bear it . . ."

-C. S. Lewis, The Magician's Nephew

Introduction

There are innumerable how-to-write-a-novel guides in the wide and wild world. So why write one more? What separates this guide from the others? First:

This book is not a guide on how to write a novel.

As the title implies and the subtitle states outright, this particular guide is specific to the possibilities while writing a <u>rough draft</u>.

Writing guides that give generalized advice or guidance on how to go from a blank page to a published story are certainly fine, and I encourage the beginning writer to read as many as they're comfortable with. However, I believe there should be a different approach to writing a rough draft as opposed to writing a complete novel, as advice meant for a final, published product may not be helpful at the beginning.

Writing a rough draft is a viscerally different experience than making edits on a final draft. A 'one size fits all' approach to this process will be less helpful one way or another. This guide, then, focuses completely on the roughest of drafts, with the idea that the writer will then go on to hire editors and continue the drafting process, applying different sets of rules and standards as their story develops.

But even more specifically, I wrote this guide to encourage potential clients to develop their rough drafts to a degree that I would consider ideal for my own services. While I'm still relatively new to the professional manuscript evaluation game, I have noticed certain aspects of storytelling that seem common, if not universal, among my clients. This guide was born from the most common areas of feedback I give to my developmental editing and beta reading clients.

You'll notice a lot of what I say here might fly in the face of standard and traditional advice on writing novels. I'm cool with that. There are no correct answers when it comes to the artistic process or even the final result. There is enough room in the art world for everyone.

To be clear, there are many writers and editors out there who may vehemently disagree with this guide. That's great! This is art, after all—if there was only one acceptable way to write, we wouldn't have the awe-inspiring breadth of literature we have today.

I do not possess the experience, nor the credentials, nor even the hubris to suggest I'm somehow the arbiter of good writing. I have no doubt there are plenty of examples of masterwork novels that don't adhere to anything I suggest here. In fact, that's one of the bigger points I want to make:

No one can tell you how to write your story.

Beyond outlining what might make a good rough draft, my aim here is to show new or relatively new indie authors how to escape the shadow that 'traditional' publishing has had on the literary arts. I'm here to help you find your voice through the art of drafting. It is offered in the spirit of support for experimentation and taking risks, to develop your art into something truly unique outside of business considerations.

Advice for rough drafts is not the same as advice for a final product.

We'll get into this more, but it's worth pointing out once more for the pedantic crowd: everything here is written with the idea that the writer is going to hire *at least one or two editors* between now and publication. Following the suggestions here for the final novel will result in an absolute mess of a manuscript. This is a guide to help you write a *rough* draft. That's it.

If the suggestions here vibe with you and you're in need of developmental editing, manuscript evaluation, or a paid beta read, feel free to reach out to me. (Contact information is at the end of the guide!) If you disagree with anything here, feel free to complain about this guide on social media—in fact, go ahead and tag me while you're at it, and I'll make sure your criticisms reach the widest possible ~~market~~ audience.

What is a Rough Draft?

There are no precise definitions of the term 'rough draft.' The concept is as varied as the writers working on them. I've seen the term used to describe anything from a handful of vague plot points to a highly polished manuscript ready for a final pass before publication.

For our purposes, I'm defining a rough draft as the first appearance of a completed story (i.e. it has a beginning, middle, and end). A completed rough draft will have had every reasonable effort made to tell a cohesive story with the understanding that this story may change significantly before publication.

In other words, the rough draft is what you would hand to a manuscript evaluator: completed enough for you to be comfortable getting feedback on it, but still early enough in the process that significant changes can be made (relatively) easily.

I'm including what might be called a first or second draft in this as well, as people who write without outlines ('discovery writers', or more commonly referred to as 'pantsers') often have no idea what their story is until they're done writing it. At that point, the pantser may go back and go through another draft simply to make everything line up and make sense. I'd consider that second draft "rough" as well, since they've arrived at approximately the same point that someone working with an outline might have on the first try.

This is in contrast to later drafts, where story elements begin to cement in place, and the emphasis moves from the story to the prose, including spelling and grammar. I leave these details in the hands of the professional line and copy editors; those brave heroes who hold the line between literary chaos and order can make the difference between good and great. Let's make sure we give them the best story we can—that way *their* talents can truly shine for the benefit of your story.

This Guide is for Indie Authors

This guide is specifically written for the independent ('indie') author who plans to self-publish their novels.

If you hope to sell your novel to a corporation, the advice here *may* be counterproductive to that goal. It simply comes down to who you're writing for. The self-published author is writing for themselves primarily, followed by their potential audiences. An indie author is only accountable to themselves and their readers.

By contrast, those seeking a corporate publishing deal must impress an agent. They will be constrained in which genres they write, the construction of their opening lines, the level of 'adult' material in their stories, and so on. There are industry standards hard-baked into the process of applying for the chance to get chosen for a book deal, and going off-script in that highly competitive market may ruin your chances of getting picked.

In other words, writing for the corporate market means constructing an ideal 'product' for a publishing company. This is a highly specific skill set that I don't possess and have no interest in. Fortunately, there are many how-to books on writing for a corporate market, so we can rest assured those seeking that path are well-supplied already.

I don't mean to be exclusionary here. Of course those writing for the trad-publishing market are more than welcome to read and see if this guide is helpful to them in their drafting process. However, I do have to make sure this disclaimer is upfront and clear, as I don't want to be blamed for agents rejecting a manuscript written with the advice of a self-publishing novelist.

(It's worth noting that you don't have to publish what you write. You can simply enjoy writing, and keep the results to yourself. This is just as valid as any form of publishing.)

Why Self-Publish?

Self-publishing is a revolution in the literary arts. The novels being published now will be studied by future graduate students as a watershed moment in literary history.

Traditionally, publishers had the final say. A corporation's only goal is to generate profit, so to a publishing corporation, novels are simply products to be marketed and sold the same way a grocery store might sell various foodstuffs. In that pursuit, deference is given to the most broadly acceptable products, with niche products often downplayed or simply not available at all. This had the unfortunate effect of silencing the creative voices of minorities and marginalized communities, as publishers often deemed these authors and stories less-profitable.

This was the status-quo until about twenty years ago, when the first print-on-demand services appeared. Without the need to fill a warehouse with books in a print run, the market doors opened wide, allowing authors to directly publish and sell their works without the need for corporate approval first.

Now that authors are free from the demands of corporate oversight, we are free to write the stories we want, however we want to write them. For better or worse, the written word has returned to a state of pure artistry. If trad-publishing is a grocery store selling mass-made prepackaged meals, an indie author is a local roadside stall or food truck—rough around the edges, but generally the better way to get riper, tastier food while supporting the local community.

With that in mind, the main thrust of this guide is to encourage experimentation free from concerns about 'the market.' As writers, we have emerged from the dark cages of sales trends to blink in the bright sunshine of self-expression. We can feel the grass under our feet with nothing but the pure breeze of inspiration rippling across endlessly wild and magical lands—with nary a fence or cage in sight.

In other words, many suggestions here may be antithetical to established writing tradition and rigidly defined 'correctness' in storytelling. I take great delight in this. There are storytelling structures, subgenres, and other literary frontiers that have yet to be explored in this new print-on-demand/ebook era. I'm beyond thrilled to have a voice to encourage writers to seek out these new and strange stories, to develop their artistry beyond the scope of stale 'traditional' publishing restrictions.

This guide is meant to be an example of the freedom afforded the writer today. Let's take a stroll through these new lands and see what strange fruits and odd beasts await.

Expectations and Final Warning

In short, the art of the rough draft is to be a pure expression of artistry in all its horrible, beautiful insanity. And again, this is *not* a guide to writing a finished, polished novel. It is not a self-publishing guide. I offer no advice or insight to anything beyond a first or second draft.

This is not a how-to guide for constructing your story or characters.

I can't ensure that what you write will be any good. There is no substitute for hard-won personal experience and talent. A writer who consistently develops and refines their writing over twenty years is likely a better writer than a young first-timer.

Sometimes writing a good novel is simply a matter of practice, experience, and study.

This guide is a foundation of drafting that would allow an editor to spend more of their time on your story, rather than addressing easily predictable shortcomings and difficulties that tend to crop up in a new writer's first attempts.

Don't worry—no amount of experience or study will prevent a writer from making mistakes. It happens to all of us. If there's a real goal here, it's to help writers make creative, unique mistakes only they are capable of, the kind that no guide can help with. That's when the true fun begins.

How To Start a Rough Draft

There's no way to start writing a novel except one: You just start writing it.

No amount of writing tips or how-to guides will make your fingers hit keys. The generally accepted definition of a novel is a book that has at least fifty thousand words, *all* of which you actually have to type.

Do you start with an outline, or are you a discovery writer? Do you start at the beginning, somewhere near the middle, or with the end first? Only you know the way that works best for you, and the only way to discover what works best is to try it. Your unique method will show itself by how you end up actually putting words to the page.

So if I can't tell you how to write your story, then what good is this guide? That's a fair question. I have to make a few assumptions about you in order to move forward. Let's lay these cards on the table right here and now: **I'm assuming you have a story that you're excited to turn into a real novel.**

The Writer at Play

The first keystroke on a blank document is a moment of ecstasy. In this moment, you begin to sing your own creation into existence. This guide is for rough drafts, and as such, it concerns itself with the sacred undertaking of *creation*. Its primary purpose is to remind the writer of the higher goals of art, to soar above and beyond the profane fields of commercialism and the endless swamps of correctness.

There is no shortage of well-meaning editors and academics giving rigidity in rules and forms. Or highly annotated textbooks with proven track records, where the forms of art and language are distilled into correctness and wrong. If you learned to read and write through school, these systems are pressed into you at the most creative age.

To engage with a purely creative space, we must unlearn the harms of academic well-meaning. Toss aside concerns for structure or grammar. Forget how we think writing "should" look. Dance among the whims of the breezes. Glide with strong currents in all their cool smoothness. Even if the waters lead you to crash upon the sharp rocks of disappointment, jump back in and try again.

Sing loud and strong. Or subtle and soft, if you prefer. It's your voice, after all. There are no teachers giving grades and no parents to disappoint—at least not yet. All of that may come later, but it is irrelevant here.

Writing a rough draft is playing, dancing with your imagination. A new universe is born with each step and twirl. Let all other considerations wait their turn. Later. After you're done dancing.

What if My Idea is Dumb?

There's no such thing as a bad idea in art. It's only a matter of executing the idea just right—in other words, whether or not you can pull off your 'dumb' idea in a way that makes it look incredible.

I'll say it again: There is no such thing as a dumb, stupid, or worthless idea when it comes to artistic self-expression. No concept is too *whatever* to be out of reach. Asking "Would anyone like to read a story about . . ." or "Do you think this is a good idea. . ." is a waste of time, because **no one can answer those questions until after the story has been written.**

This is your rough draft, not your final document. No one but an editor or evaluator is going to read it. Professionals you're paying for professional feedback don't care how ridiculous the premise is or the characters are, a professional is going to take your work seriously.

Look at the premise behind some of the most famous stories today:

- A magical farm boy gets recruited by a space wizard to rescue a princess from an evil robot-man.

- Magic jewelry needs to be tossed in a volcano or else the world will end.

- Sentient car aliens rescue earth from other sentient car aliens.

What determines a pile of crap from a masterpiece isn't the idea behind it—it's entirely based on how well the artist managed to turn the idea into something incredible. Start with stupid ideas, then dare yourself to make them stupider. This is the path of the rough draft.

Inspiration Types

This might be a controversial statement, but I believe the first step in writing a story is to be inspired. I believe in the magic of an artist's holy moment of insight and excitement, when the idea arrives in the same manner of being struck by lightning, leaving them wide-eyed, mouth agape as the universe downloads something incredible right into their soul.

I'm making a distinction between two different types of inspiration, as sometimes these terms can be confusing. We'll call one type a 'moment' and the other a 'state.'

Moment of Inspiration

This is the lightning bolt. More often than not, this occurs at the least appropriate times—driving, shopping, while at work, sitting on the toilet, you name it.

This is often the story artists talk about when asked how they came up with the premise for their work. It's always a story of some kind: "It was the dead of winter and I pulled up to a stop sign. A certain song was on the radio, and suddenly I could see . . ."

This is an ideal way to start a project. Having an idea for a story is approximately 0.01% of the work required to write a novel, but don't get the wrong idea—without that tiny bit, the other 99.99% wouldn't be possible.

State of Inspiration

Writing in a state of inspiration is the writer's ideal. Often called the 'flow' or similar terms, it's when everything seems to line up perfectly. Your fingers can barely keep up with the words as they flow effortlessly out of you and onto the page.

While this is certainly the most fun way to write, it is often a fleeting feeling that is hard to replicate. For our purposes, we don't need to be in this state to write. You certainly can wait until you feel this way, as long as you embrace the fact that doing so can turn a six-month writing process into a decades-long one. You might find that the greater enjoyment in only writing when you feel inspired outweighs a productive 'grind' mindset. On the other hand, the joy of being able to publish novel after novel might yield a greater joy, one that outweighs the frustration and burnout of being productive all the time.

As an indie author, you set the pace. You alone set the expectations for your production rate, as well as your final quality. There's no wrong way to do it, except one: the way that makes you miserable. Any system that doesn't make you miserable and allows you to write freely will work, at least as far as rough drafts are concerned.

Do You Need Inspiration to Start?

In case you couldn't tell, my approach to writing is that it is an art first. It can be a business, of course, but to approach your rough draft from the mindset of producing products for sale is so damn depressing. So, yes, I believe you should be *inspired* to start writing your story. It's frankly inconceivable that anyone could write an entire novel without being inspired somehow—where do the ideas come from, if not that place of artistic awe?

It may be difficult to trigger that inspiring moment. Some might argue that it's not up to us at all, that inspiration works according to its own rules and whims. The muses bless and curse as they will. As such, I have no advice on how to get inspired. I imagine that every human being has their own ways and means to achieve some feeling of inspiration. Do that (so long as it's healthy) as often as you can, and see if you can stretch and exercise those inspiration muscles.

Your passion is the fuel that will push you through the muck of drafting. Your excitement for your story will flow from your words to the reader, a shocking charge capable of zapping anyone who comes into contact with your art. Done right, your readers will love your story at least as much as you do—if not more!

There are plenty of well-meaning 'professional' writers and business-people who will tell you to disregard your inspiration, that writing a story is a set path that requires consistent work and nothing else. They are correct in the sense that consistency is vital to writing a novel, but I disagree with the casual dismissal of inspiration. Art without inspiration is a body without a soul.

Writing a novel can absolutely be one of the hardest undertakings, but it also can be indescribably joyful and fulfilling. This guide leans heavily in favor of enjoying the process over having a professional manuscript—because, again, *we're only writing a rough draft*, not a novel. Why wouldn't you want your rough draft to be everything you want? Why approach your rough draft with caution and restraint? The public is never going to read it!

Understanding that the rough draft is a safe space to explore your own creativity is the whole point of this book. Get that in your head and heart now, and the rest of this will make a lot more sense. Probably.

So how do you start a rough draft? **Just start typing out your inspiration without a worry in the world.** Rest assured those worries are coming later by way of editors and drafts, but the more you feel free to explore your story and characters in the beginning, the more delightful the final product will be.

The Birthday Party Method

Think of your rough draft like a birthday party that your inner child always wanted, but *more.*

Most of us have an idea of what a good birthday party might have: a cake, presents, maybe a bouncy castle if your parents have money. Here, however, we are not constrained by realistic considerations. *This is the birthday party you always wanted in the depths of your childlike imagination.* This party is unconstrained by reality in every possible way—the limit is simply your ability to imagine.

You want to have it in a castle? Imagine the coolest castle ever. Who cares about realistic castles for the time and place—you're a child, you want the *coolest* castle, period. You want all your friends to come? Not only them, but also your favorite characters from your favorite movies, comics, and so on. Your favorite band doesn't just play Happy Birthday—they get into a battle of the bands with your other favorite band to win your favor.

However, **no one is invited to this party.** Not yet, anyway. There may be some concern of embarrassment if your guests arrive and there's simply too much for them to handle, or if the decorations clash, or whatever else that works with this analogy.

Fortunately, we're writing a *rough* draft. Rough drafts are not for the public, they are very private documents. It is vital to keep in mind that no one is going to read your rough draft—no one except your editor, who will help refine your unlimited imagination into something truly awesome.

The most important part of this concept is that everyone will develop a party that showcases who they are in the most unique way. In real life, a birthday party might cater to the base interests of the 'child demographic' in a generic way. In *your* party, not only do you get to define it according to your passions, you also get to invite friends who share those same passions.

So instead of thinking about what kind of birthday cake you'd get, really consider what your version of an ideal birthday party could be—maybe it's a knitting party with your favorite characters who delight in each other's company and share your favorite tea. Maybe it's a quest to slay an evil dragon-wizard with laser-cannons and flying pickup trucks.

What's your ideal party? And by that I mean: What's your most-fun story with all the coolest stuff? The only person saying 'no' to your ideas is *you*. If you find yourself denying yourself the coolest ideas for your story, ask yourself why. Is it because it's not that cool? Or is it some internalized ideal of what a story *should* be?

A birthday party can be anything that the birthday-haver would want, so **Happy Birthday** and invite your editor to the most wild, fun, satisfying party you're capable of imagining.

Let your joy and excitement guide your fingers on the keyboard first. We can always become dull, disappointing adults who talk about practicality later—that's what the editing process is for. But for right now? Your rough draft should dance in the delight of unfettered self-expression. It should follow the winds of passion across the lands of imagination, soaring and diving at your slightest whim. Play with the words, the characters, the structure. Your editor will highlight the parts that need to be fixed, so don't do their job for them. Your job is to write.

No blocks can stop your writing if it truly flows freely, as water flows around or seeps through any obstacle, your creativity can overcome our inherited limitations in the most grand and dramatic fashion. Probably.

Now, let's get into some of the most common issues I see in rough drafts. The more aware you are of these elements at the onset, the easier it'll be to weave them into your inspiration—and thereby, the easier your overall writing journey will be.

In Summary

Play first, work later. Be inspired, even if you have to reach to find your inspiration. Fill your rough draft with everything you've got. Think about it from every angle. A rough draft is not the time for limitations or timidity. This is the time to be as big and bold as you are capable of. We can always reduce and refine in later drafts, so start off with gusto!

Plot

Obviously, I can't tell you what the plot of your story is going to be. And since this is a rough draft, you may not know what it'll be either. Let's face it, this section is going to be pretty short.

However, it is worth keeping some basic ideas in mind while slinging words on paper. In a nutshell: How your main characters interact with mystery determines the shape of your plot. The shape of your plot defines your genre. Any setting can be applied to any genre, so the setting of your story can be whatever tickles your fancy.

Genre and Setting

The term 'genre' should refer to the primary *structure* of the story. This is different from a story's setting. Typically, a story has one primary genre, but it can have any number of different settings.

For example, a story about a detective trying to find *whodunit* can take place in a contemporary setting. It can also take place in a fantasy setting, or a science fiction one. But it can't take place in a horror setting, because there's no such thing as a horror *setting*—horror is a genre that, as you might guess, can also take place in any setting. (A detective in a horror novel is going to follow the structure of a horror novel, even if they're doing detective work.)

Genres are most typically only one per story. Trying to blend genres is like trying to push repelling magnets together. It's a hard and frustrating task, as different types of stories have different structures that may not fit together.

Blending settings, however, is always rad as hell. **Settings are the hats your characters and world wear.** Science fiction is *not* a genre—it's a setting. Actors can act the same Shakespear play in front of ten thousand different backgrounds, each lending a flavor, but none changing the story itself. In the same way, a space explorer can trade in her helmet for a hooded fantasy cloak without skipping a single story beat (spaceships become sailing ships, aliens become strange peoples, planets are islands, etc).

Settings can include: science fiction, fantasy, historical, dystopian, post-apocalyptic, magical realism, and western. So if you set out to write a western, you'll still need to figure out what story structure it'll have. You'll still need to determine the *genre*.

Settings are not stories.

This is why it's important to know the difference even before you start writing. Your plot structure is the shape of your story, the path your characters follow, and the genre/category your story will end up in. The setting you choose for your story is the icing on the cake. It's what people see first when they look at it, but it can hide what lies beneath, which is why we categorize cakes by what's under the icing first.

Knowing this distinction can help you figure out where a storytelling weakness may lie, or inspire you to change locations on a whim. Since this is your rough draft, you may discover that your romance might be a little more fun if it took place on a spaceship instead of a castle. Knowing your *story* remains safe as the aesthetics switch could lead to some incredibly exciting discoveries about your story, and maybe even some discoveries about yourself.

Unfortunately, our current genre classification system is a mess. There are more genres than the ones I talk about here, but hopefully you can see how I approach this issue, so you can apply this idea to whatever genre you want to write in.

It's worth noting that all of this is very much my own system. Amazon has their own idea of what a 'genre' is. Fortunately we don't have to worry about Amazon just yet—we're only writing the rough draft!

Let's take a look at some examples and see if we can figure all this out. Most genres have a typical twist at the end of the second act, so I've included some descriptions of what those might be as well. (All these examples have corresponding shapes, so maybe someday I can have an illustrated version.)

Romance

The mystery of a romance is how these two (or more) people who aren't together at the start get together by the end. Imagine a circle with a ? inside, which we'll call the 'mystery.'

In a romance, two or more main characters enter the mystery from different angles. Friends to lovers might enter the mystery close together, while enemies to lovers would enter the circle from opposing sides. The mystery of the plot is how these characters overcome their personal difficulties to exit that circle happily together.

For the twist, inside the mystery circle is *another* circle, inside of which the two (or more) main characters break up, distance themselves, have a fight, or whatever else casts the obviously inevitable ending into doubt. The conflict isn't necessarily against an external opponent—the primary villain of a romance could be the character's own flaws coming back to haunt them.

In any case, the outcome is the same—the two (or more) characters leave the conflict zone, re-enter the mystery circle once more, and then arrive outside at the end, now firmly together.

Romance is the one genre that really understands the distinction between genre and setting. There's no shortage of romance novels of any setting imaginable, but each is structured in such a way that anyone who reads it can say 'Yup, this is a romance novel."

Adventure

Oh, my darling genre has been neglected and misunderstood for far too long. Righting this injustice is a personal goal of mine, so you best believe I'm going to define this genre as something unique and separate from Action right here and now.

An Adventure story is a journey through a new and magical land in search of something important. The shape of the Adventure genre is a long, thin mystery circle that represents a new location. The hero engages in the mystery by traveling through these strange new worlds in their search for the plot object (usually just a MacGuffin).

The twist comes from a sudden disaster of some kind—travel plans go awry, supplies are lost, perhaps even the characters themselves are lost. The ferocity of this new world bares its fangs at the hero(s), and they have to learn how to snarl right back to survive.

Lumping this genre with Action was a crime against the arts. Adventure is its own genre, shoulder to shoulder with Romance both in terms of legitimacy and tradition. It has fallen out of favor over the years due mainly to outdated character tropes, but I think this genre is primed for a true comeback.

Action/Detective/Mystery

I lumped all these together because they all have the same story shape, and are thereby almost indistinguishable from each other in terms of plot structure. The only difference between action and detective is the action hero uses their fists to advance, while the detective uses their wits.

The image is of another mystery circle. The hero interacts with the mystery by forcing their way through it. The circle pushes back, but the hero persists, and in doing so, discovers the twist: a second, deeper mystery that the hero must stop before it's too late. Whether that's setting up a trap for the villain before they leave, or running across town to save someone, one of the hallmarks of this genre is the relatively slow pacing at the start, only to come crashing down on a final action scene.

The Action genre is different from Adventure in a number of ways, but chief among them is that an Action story can take place in any location, while Adventure is usually limited to a 'new' location, as the delight of discovery is the hallmark of Adventure. Action, by contrast, can be enhanced by the main character being familiar and experienced with the story's location.

Horror

In a reverse of the others, the horror genre mystery actually seeks out the hero instead of waiting for the hero's lead. Typically, it's the hero's fault for triggering the mystery, although rarely by design. The hero then spends most of the story trying to avoid or run from the mystery.

The twist comes when the hero has been pushed past their fears and limitations. When that happens, the hero turns around to face the mystery head-on. This is a very predator/prey dynamic, and the reversals of those roles leads directly to confrontation and (relative) victory.

Taking up a classic example of a mystery monster hunting the hero, we can see that this idea could play out over any number of settings. A monster hiding in a house can easily be an alien monster on a spaceship, or a sea-dwelling monster on a fantasy ship, or a mythological monster-bear hunting some cowboys.

In Summary

While I could fill a book with the discussion of genres and settings, this should be all we really need to start a rough draft. There are sub-categories of sub-sub-categories to be discovered, but to be honest, don't worry too much about selecting a genre or setting just yet.

Ultimately, how your book is categorized is other people's concern, not yours. Just write your story exactly how you want it to be. Write freely in your story structure, but keeping your mind open to a change of venue to combat potential blocks and difficulties is all we need here.

Stakes

The single most oft-repeated feedback my clients get is about the *stakes of their story*. I can't over-emphasize how important clearly defined stakes are to hooking a reader. What is at stake here? Fortunately, finding those story-stakes is easy. All you need to do is answer a very simple question:

What will happen if the main character fails?

The answer, simply stated, is the stake of your primary plot. Not only that, it also answers the first question a potential reader has when they first pick up a book: *Why should I care what happens here?*

Story stakes broadly fall under two categories:
- **External** (The stakes occur outside of the character in the wider world.)

- **Internal** (The stakes are personal and emotional in nature.)

Regardless of your genre, I suggest having *at least one of each per main character*. Some readers will vibe more with one than the other, so having both allows your story to appeal to the widest possible audience without sacrificing your artistic integrity in the process.

Also, having both internal and external stakes ties the story's world to your main character's personal journey, and vice versa. It allows for a significant amount of flexibility on how you get to your ending. It gives your characters depth and motivation as they engage in the plot.

Setting up these stakes as early as possible gives the reader a sense of urgency. You don't have to state it outright (although that always helps). How you approach showing the stakes of the story will depend entirely on your writing style. In any case, I **strongly** suggest aiming to have the reader at least vaguely aware of the story-stakes by the end of the first chapter.

In case I wasn't clear before, **knowing the stakes of your story is foundational to writing the plot.** Without *something* at stake, there's no reason for anyone to read your story, and no reason for your characters to live through it. A story in which the hero fails and nothing happens isn't a story, it's just a series of events.

I could go on about this all day, but hopefully you can see how important this is. Write down the answer to that simple question, both internally and externally, and do so for each main character—heck, feel free to do it for *all* of your characters. Refer back to those answers frequently while writing, and even your roughest draft may end up more compelling than half the books on bookstore shelves right now.

Internal/External

The actual stakes themselves depend significantly on the genre you're writing. Your genre not only defines what kind of story structure you're writing, but also who the majority of your readers will be.

Again, speaking broadly, your internal stakes are often what makes your characters relatable. Your average reader may not know what it feels like to save an entire planet from destruction, but all of them will know what it feels like to overcome a personal difficulty of some kind—heartbreak, trauma, anxiety, loneliness, and all the rest.

This is yet another great reason to let your imagination run wild at the onset. As long as your story is anchored in some intimately internal stakes, your external stakes could be wildly outlandish and people will praise your characters as 'relatable' even if the story takes place ten thousand years in the future and deep in outer space, or in a fantasy land with magical elves, or anywhere your imagination is capable of conjuring—including our contemporary modern-day.

Let's take up a few examples from different genres and explore how they might approach their stakes. Remember the question: What happens if the main character fails?

Romance

External: The Main Character A (MC-A) is a widower who needs help running his family store while he juggles being a single dad and small business owner.

Internal: The MC-A is having difficulty handling his grief, leading to him shutting his feelings off, thereby harming his relationship with his children.

In this example, there are two clearly defined stakes: He might lose the shop his grandpa built if the business fails, and he risks losing his relationship with his children unless he learns how to feel again. The second main character (MC-B) comes into the story to resolve both of these stakes, while at the same time bringing their own set of external/internal stakes that MC-A can help resolve for them.

Adventure

External: A young person must travel to a strange fantasy land to collect a special flower to save their beloved from a magical illness.

Internal: The young person struggles to believe in themselves and is terrified of letting down the one person who needs them the most.

In this example, the magical flower is simply a MacGuffin around which the story's struggles take place. Not getting the flower isn't *just* a failure to save a beloved, it's a personal failure for the main character. Your readers are naturally going to cheer your MC on through those tough times, as fearing failure is an intimately relatable situation, even if traveling through fantasy lands may not be a common, relatable situation for the average reader.

Action

External: Someone important to the main character is kidnapped and held hostage by a fearsome gang. The main character must rescue them before it's too late.

Internal: The main character has lost someone important to them before by being too weak. They can't handle the possibility of losing another—doing so again would destroy their soul.

While the Action genre typically emphasizes the external stakes, you may notice that nearly every good action-genre story spends a great deal of time explaining the hero's traumatic backstory and such. These story devices show that the internal state of the hero drives the action. Combined with the external conflict, this can make a very compelling mix of motivation and emotion amongst the explosion and punches and whatnot.

Without those personal stakes, the action can fall flat. The audience/readers will be wondering *why* this character is undergoing such effort and injury during what should be the most impactful fight of the story. It'd be a lot easier to just . . . not do all that fighting, right? The internal stake of failure is the motivation of your characters. The external stake of the story is the plot. Or something like that.

In Summary

Any compelling story is going to have a main character with both an internal and external stake in the story's outcome.

Having only one big stake that influences the world at large without any personal stakes from the hero will leave readers wondering why your hero is going through all this trouble at all.

On the other hand, a purely internal motivation without any stakes in the outside world may make justifying your hero's actions difficult, as they'll risk coming across as selfish or delusional.

In other words, punching someone because you're feeling bad on the inside is horrible, but punching someone to save someone else (*despite* you feeling bad on the inside) is heroic. The internal stake is character motivation, the external stake is the plotline.

Narrative Framing

Is your story told from a first-person perspective, or third? What are the pros and cons of each? How would you be able to tell if your story is one or the other? What about tense? Is there a larger framework that your story fits into?

One of the more interesting things that can happen is the realization that a story was written in the wrong perspective. More than once I've done an evaluation on a story written in the third person, only to suddenly understand that the story being told is actually a first-person story.

One of the strongest recommendations I can make for helping a rough draft along is to develop the willingness to try something different. After all, **one of the best parts of writing a rough draft is that we're free to experiment** whenever and however the mood hits. I encourage you to deviate from what you might *believe* your story is any time you get the feeling it might be something different.

For example: Halfway through your third-person rough draft, you have a sudden suspicion that your story might be better in the first person. Looking into the possibility is as easy as typing your next paragraph in the first person point of view and seeing for yourself. If you like it, write the next paragraph that way as well. If it works and you see now that your story was supposed to be in the first person all along, then you only have *half* a rough draft to fix now, instead of fixing the entire manuscript when you might have realized this later.

Knowing the correct perspective will have a significant impact on the story you're telling—and it's the rough draft's role to make sure you land in the right place for your story as early as possible.

Experimentation in a rough draft can lead to some significant discoveries about your story, and perhaps even about yourself. Given that the whole thing is going to be rewritten anyway, there's nothing to lose and everything to gain. You're a mad scientist bringing this cobbled-together corpse to life. Greatness awaits!

First Person versus Third Person

It's worth taking a moment and asking yourself what type of story you're actually writing. We all have our personal bias towards one or the other, but I believe the story itself dictates point of view and tense in the same way shapes and colors might dictate the emotion and story of a painting.

In other words, the *type* of story being told prefers one or the other, even if you personally don't. Here's a quick guide on how to determine which might be right for your tale.

Third Person POV

Does your story involve more than one main character? Does the span and scope of your tale often take a larger view of the factors in play? Does the story easily switch between characters, or even take time outside of the story itself to describe situations and events that none of the characters are aware of?

Third person shines most in stories that involve a wide scope of consideration. These are situations where the story's emphasis is less on the internal impact of the story and more on the externalities. I recommend it when writing about a diverse cast of characters, where the world plays a large role, when the locations and situations vary greatly, and so on.

The drawback of this style is that it lacks a degree of intimacy. The reader and the main character remain separate people, which makes it easier to distance oneself from the story.

Limited versus Omniscient

This consideration plays a greater role later in the drafting process, but it's worth mentioning quickly.

As the name implies, limited third person is like the first person point of view, except it's in the third. The story is intimately from this one character's perspective, which limits what the character knows about the story and other characters. The world and characters around the main character could be described from this character's own values and biases.

Omniscient, on the other hand, is unlimited in scope and knowledge. We can pass between characters, fly deep into outer space, whatever the narrator wants. The story could be filled with information that none of the characters know, leading to some potentially interesting drama and tension, like the reader shouting at a character to try and warn them through the page.

Choosing which one you want for your story will most likely take some experimentation. For this, I suggest writing one chapter with one, then another the other way. Again, the type of story you're trying to tell should determine which of these two is the better fit for giving the reader the stakes.

First Person POV

Does your story strictly adhere to one character? Does the internal monologue and emotional state of your main character make up a large portion of the story? Does your main character have thoughts and feelings that no one but the reader can see?

By obvious contrast, the first person point of view excels at telling a very personal, intimate story. Internal dialogue, feelings, personal reactions other character's can't see—this is where the first person shines. Having the reader join with your character in the statement of "I" and "My" can create an emotional impact that might be difficult to achieve in third.

The drawback of this style is that it makes telling the wider story more difficult. Locked into a singularly character perspective, any information about the wider world still has to filter through this perspective. That makes telling a wide-scope story with lots of characters a challenge.

Central/Side

Is your main character the hero of your story, or are they a character who observes from the side? Many classic tales are told by someone who was there when it happened, someone who bore witness to the hero's grand sacrifice. Or perhaps a friend, telling a story about the hero to show their audience the humanity behind the fables.

Sometimes it's easier to tell a story by standing to the side and letting the events take place, where the main character of the plot isn't the main character of the story. This can add a layer of nuance and complexity, giving some depth to what might otherwise seem rote or unoriginal.

Like everything else, which you choose will depend largely on your story, or more accurately, on that moment of inspiration that got you started.

Reliable/Unreliable

While an unreliable third person narrator is just a liar, an unreliable first person narrator has the potential for some real story shenanigans. However, the difficulty of telling a fulfilling character-driven story with an unreliable narrator is extreme. You effectively end up with two concurrent stories—one real, one a lie. This is the kind of thing that generally requires a lot of outlining and planning, so this is a bit outside of the more generalized advice here. I wish you good luck!

Present Tense versus Past Tense

Much like first/third person considerations, deciding on which tense to use may depend more on the type of story being told than personal preference. That said, it has been my experience that readers can react strongly to a particular type of tense with even more love or hate than the first/third person.

But since we have no control over how people react to your story, this is one area where personal preference can be your guiding light. It all comes down to the sense of urgency you want to give the reader. In other words, **this is mostly a question of style.**

Past Tense

Past tense is often considered the default for novels. Most of us are familiar with it from reading 'the classics' while growing up. There is a sizable contingent who consider past tense to be more 'correct' than present tense, and dedicated past-tensers might toss your book the moment they realize it's in present tense. You can write in past tense well assured that almost no one is going to talk about your choice to do so. It is the safest of bets.

Narratively speaking, past tense does imply everything in the story already happened, as opposed to it happening right now. A good writer can overcome this and give that urgency in a past tense story of course, but it takes extra skill to do so.

Present Tense

The rise of present tense is one of the hallmarks of modern publishing. As authors are no longer constrained to academics and publishing standards, telling a tale as it's happening has become an increasingly popular choice with both indie and corporately-published books. Some dismiss it as something of a fad (or worse), while others celebrate its continuing rise in modern fiction.

Obviously this is the opposite of past tense in all respects. The story the reader is reading didn't happen—it's happening *right now*. Add in a first-person perspective and you've got the most potent framing to give your readers a panic attack.

I urge caution when using present tense as, again, there are a significant number of readers who dislike it. Play around and make sure it fits within the overall vibe of the story you're telling. There's a reason you often see present tense paired with first person, as that makes a cohesive and faster-paced experience of one character's journey. Using it in the third person is purely a stylistic choice; as far as I can see, there's no objective benefit gained for doing so.

Ultimately, this is a choice you have to make for yourself. **I strongly encourage you to experiment** with both as you write your first draft, and by the end you should have no doubt which is right for the story you want to tell.

Meta World Building

This section is entirely optional, but I believe it's worth considering as there's nothing at risk for the attempt. Isn't writing a rough draft great? You can do whatever you want!

Self-referential framing is often neglected by first-time writers, as it can add a layer of complexity to a story you might already be struggling to tell. Having your story be told by another character, or having it be a written record found somewhere, or any of the myriad possibilities that can surround a story, does run narrative risks.

However, they can also provide *relief* from storytelling troubles that might not have an elegant solution. A good narrative frame can turn what would have been a boring lore-dump into a fun bonus story. Done right, this extra bit of storytelling can go a long way in framing the events and characters in your story beyond the scope of the story itself.

This is effectively a sort of secondary storyline that takes place above and around your primary storyline. Like the primary story, it's only limit is your imagination. Some authors will write poems or song lyrics that turn their stories into something more epic. Others might use the in-between chapter space to quote some in-world textbook or holy scripture about a location, character, or monster type. The type of story you're writing will naturally lend itself to certain types of framing that fit best within your genre and storytelling vibe.

Since we're working with no limitations in this rough draft, I strongly suggest a gleeful experimentation with the meta narrative foundation. You have your story, sure, but who is telling this story, and to whom? Answering those questions can uncover another layer to your tale and make you look like you really know what you're doing.

Examples

There is no limit to the possibilities here, so I encourage you to think of your own unique situations. **These are just a few examples to stimulate the imagination.**

The Scholar

The scholar is a classic meta-narrative device. From actively interviewing a primary source to spending their lives translating the ancient scrolls and texts, the scholar's entire existence is in bringing the story to the reader, often with their own footnotes and comments added in.

The scholar often frames the story as a report of some kind, either for a library or university's records, or as a series of missives to a mysterious benefactor who funded the endeavor. And just for funsies, the scholar can also have their own little side-plot as a treat.

Having an easy way to do some worldbuilding or lore dumping in a way that flows naturally with the story structure can be a fun way to give the reader a bit of a mental and emotional cleansing moment. You can also add footnotes in the scholar's voice, again enhancing your ability to explain without taking the reader completely out of the story.

The potential drawbacks of this is that it could remove the story's sense of urgency. Past tense already implies the story already happened, but having a nerd translate an ancient scroll in a dusty library truly implies that nothing in the story actually matters to the here-and-now.

The Storyteller

A more active form of a scholar is the classic troubadour tale. This can be told over a campfire, in a rowdy inn, or anywhere with a captive audience. Sometimes this takes the form of an *interrogation*, where one of the characters from your story is telling what happened to a potentially hostile audience. Or the storyteller can use the tale to explain how the heroes of yore were failable people with troubles and flaws, to show the naive listeners the dangers of idolization.

Since the storyteller is actively telling the story, this allows for some back-and-forth from the audience. That interaction gives you the option to insert clarifications on events, or even humorous commentary on a character's actions ("He did *what*? What a moron!").

The Journal or Letter

A blend of scholar and storyteller, the journal/letter setup is another good way to frame a story in a personal and intimate way. This is difficult to pull off if your prose is the third person, since most journals are written in the first. This can be a pure journal-story, or your story can be interspersed with excerpts from a character reflecting back on the story from a later time.

Like the storyteller, this method gives you the option for self-reflection from someone in the world. Hindsight being what it is, a character can be anything from mournful to wistful to enraged to a divine sense of acceptance as they reflect on what happened long ago. This allows you to add in a layer of color and complexity to what might otherwise be a simple tale.

In Summary

As we've seen, there are a lot of options when it comes to how you frame your story. Some might say too many to consider for what is just a first rough draft, but *nay*, I say. Nay! Not too much! Not enough!

Remember that there is nothing at stake for your rough draft, so rather than be overwhelmed with possibilities, simply remind yourself that **you are free to experiment if and when you so choose**. We all know the frustrations that can arise in telling a story—when that happens, take a look at this section and see if there's something here that can light your path forward. You may be surprised by what your story actually wants to be if you give it the space to develop itself. Give yourself a taste of all the flavors the literary arts have to offer before settling down to write your second draft masterpiece.

Show and Tell

The most standard and oft-repeated writer's 'rule' is **Show, Don't Tell.**

But why? And what does that mean, exactly? Let's get into Show Don't Tell, and then let's talk about when Tell, Don't Show might be more appropriate.

Show, Don't Tell

I've personally said "Show Don't Tell!" more times than I care to count, and I stand by every one of them. However, it is difficult to follow a rule that isn't self-evident, leaving many a newbie writer scrambling in the dark.

Showing is the way you tell your readers something by describing something else.

That's about as clear as mud, so let's break it down with some examples. See if you can spot where this rule might not be the best choice.

Tell: He was angry.

Show: His face turned red as he scowled deeply.

In this example, I don't tell you he's angry. I show you his face and his reaction, leaving the reader to extrapolate his emotional state. The benefit here is in the flexibility the reader has in their interpretations—they are free to apply a deeper, richer emotional state than simple anger.

Tell: She was really happy.

Show: She jumped up and down clapping as her smile stretched her cheeks to redness.

Showing actions over telling emotions makes your story feel more vibrant and alive. Instead of trying to guess how this character looks when she's happy, we instead see her acting as one might expect a happy person to. Again, this gives the reader more room to apply depth to the moment—perhaps this show of excitement and glee masks a deeper feeling?

Tell: There was an apple on the table.

Show: The early morning sun shone across the kitchen table with only the long-cast shadow of an apple to divide the golden rays.

By describing an environment more broadly, the reader will be able to more clearly visualize a scene. An apple on a table could look like anything, from beautiful to disgusting. It is poetic rather than factual, as showing the reader the entire scene invites the reader to see themselves there in that moment of light and darkness.

Tell: Suddenly, a man appeared.

Show: Broad shoulders seemed to arrive from nowhere, as all at once the outline of a tall, muscular man stood before her.

The arrival of an unexpected character in a dramatic moment is inevitably going to be a vitally important moment in your plot. These keystone moments should stand out in the reader's mind with all the power and showmanship we can bring to the table—and that means describing the hell out of it.

When I say "show, don't tell" I mean specifically for those moments where a description of something conveys more gravitas and meaning than simply pointing it out. This is one of the hallmarks of a good writer, especially when it comes to conveying deep and complex emotions.

Simply stating an emotional response, character arrival, or other important scenes to the reader precludes nuance and reads as a frankly immature or inexperienced writer's attempt to tell a story. *Showing*, on the other hand, provides the illusion of depth. As the reader fills in those details, they will credit the writer for being just so good at the whole writing thing.

Tell, Don't Show

Hopefully, by now you see that this advice has a limited application in storytelling. It would be impractical at best to 'show' anything conceptual in nature. Stories can contain multitudes of conceptual ideas that would be impossible (or highly impractical) to show.

Let's grab a few examples to think about.

Tell: Six months passed without any real progress to show for it.

Show: ???

I honestly have no idea how to *show* six months passing without several paragraphs of environmental descriptions. While that could be a more poetic option, sometimes the reader just wants to know what happens next. You don't always have to show things, especially story beats that have no obvious way of being shown at all.

Tell: Without the tools to fix the engine, the ship was dead in the water.

Show: ???

Again, it may be difficult to impossible to show a reader an abstract concept. You can describe the engine all you want, and you can show the ship not going anywhere, but tying the two points together in a way that the reader doesn't have to decipher might be the better choice. It's more than OK to just come out and say things like this, especially if it makes the overall story flow better.

Tell: There was an apple on the table.

Show: The early morning light shone across the kitchen table with only the long-cast shadow of an apple to divide the golden rays.

I use this example again because sometimes the story doesn't need a lengthy description of a scene. At times you might find it's better to simply state something outright. And while showing can give a scene depth and nuance, telling can give an emotional moment more 'punch.' In this example, if the buildup to this moment works right, simply reading "there was an apple on the table" could cause your readers to cry, or laugh, or have any other strong emotional reaction—and much more so than the alternative 'show' line.

In other words, **'telling' is the best way to convey a lot of information quickly.** It's also the best way to get through a part of your story that doesn't require the reader to be immersed in a scene or event.

Technically, all stories are telling. You're telling your readers something even if it counts as 'showing,' so drawing a line between telling and showing is really a fool's errand. The whole point of this is that *sometimes* it's a good idea to show your readers something, and just as often it's a good idea to simply tell your readers something.

In truth, it takes *both* showing and telling to work together to build your best work. The skill comes from knowing when and where to apply each. If done correctly, a story will flow easily while being evocative and engaging.

As a general rule, new and inexperienced authors struggle the most with showing over telling, so the rule 'show don't tell' has embedded itself in the writing profession as some sort of nebulous guideline that people love to hate.

BUT WAIT, THIS IS JUST A ROUGH DRAFT! Why should a writer spend time working on showing/telling when this is just a first stab at getting the words on the page?

I'll keep saying it for as many times as it takes: rough drafts are *the* time for experimentation. Keep showing and telling in mind as you write, and ask yourself often: Is this something to show, or tell? Play around with it, use them in unexpected ways, learn your particular style through these elements. You neve know what you might uncover in your own story by taking a minute to show instead of tell . . . and you never know how you might tighten up your story by telling instead of showing. If you have *fun* with it, then it will never be a waste of time.

Descriptions

One of the most consistent issues I see with rough drafts is the lack of descriptions.

Which descriptions specifically depend on the author, as each has their own strengths and weaknesses. That said, everyone has blind spots, so here is a brief rundown of different types of descriptions, why they're important, and some suggestions on how to think about them.

Reader's Needs

Think of your readers as brains in jars. Devoid of their sensory organs, they cannot see, nor hear, nor smell, taste, or even feel. They know nothing, sense nothing, and live in a void—not even black or white, but simply the absence of all things. The only point of contact with the outside world: your keyboard.

These brain-jars can only experience the sensations that you describe to them. They cannot see inside your mind. If you see a character clearly in your head but you don't describe that character in writing, not one reader will ever *see* that character—all they'll see, if anything, is a blank outline with the character's name inside.

In other words, descriptions make the difference between being told a story and *living* that story. Your readers want to live in your world. They want to smell your characters! Writers contain universes in their mind filled with brilliant worlds and colorful characters—and it's your job to make sure the readers get to see those elements on the page.

Sentences as Brushstrokes

I made a fuss about not caring about grammar or spelling at the start of this guide, and I stand by that. However, it is worth mentioning: the stronger your sentence game is, the easier the writing (and editing) process will be.

The way I like to discuss prose is as an allegory, which should be no surprise at this point, given this guide is basically nothing but allegories: Think of each sentence as a brush stroke on a canvas. There are natural moments that arise in a story where a single sentence can be brought out and highlighted—if done right, this can add to the story and impress your readers all in one go.

What kind of brush you use, the colors you use, these are all stylistic choices. Variety is also important—if all sentences had the same length and strength, the work would become monotonous at best. Variation is vital. Some sentences can be a beautiful showcase of talent. But if every sentence is like that, the overall image you're painting can get lost in the flowery, self-indulgence of showing off.

Conversely, without any attention paid to the artistry of your sentences, the overall image can appear dull, even if the image itself is of something theoretically exciting.

I suggest practicing writing sentences the same way a painter might practice their brushstrokes. Scrap paper and a pen is all you need to get started. Outside of your rough draft, the stakes are even lower, so allow yourself to make colossal sentence-structuring mistakes as you investigate the kinds of word-flows you enjoy the most. This is an artistic skill like any other, and as such, practice, review, feedback, study, and more practice can yield incredible results.

Purple Prose

There's a lot of bad advice out there about not writing "purple prose" or overloading your reader with too many details and descriptions. While there may be some merit to this in terms of your final product, this 'advice' to avoid purple prose is *terrible* when it comes to writing your rough draft.

There's no limit to the number and type of descriptions you can put in your rough draft.

As an editor, *I'd vastly prefer to have too many* and spend my time suggesting cuts, rather than endlessly repeating variations of "I'd love to see a description of this castle" or "What does this character look like?"

I don't just want purple prose—I want your *ultraviolet* prose.

Having more to work with in the editing and drafting process means those descriptions have the opportunity to 'marinate.' In other words, the sooner these descriptions are in your drafts, the more likely they are to take on more significance to the overall story. What might start out as just a character's coat color can take on deep personal significance and have a profound impact on the final product if given time to be worked into the flow.

Again: I'm not here to tell you how to write. If you prefer to save your descriptions until much later in the process, that's entirely up to you. Just know your editor would rather have them sooner than later, and you run the risk of your descriptions seeming to be disconnected from the story—an annoying aside thrown in to appease picky readers, rather than integral to the story itself.

But **when** is a good time to put descriptions in your story? I'm so glad you asked—that's the next section!

If 'New,' Then Describe.

If it's new, it needs a description. A new character arrives? Show us what they look like. Your character makes it to a new location? Show us this new place. (And I don't just mean visually—I mean all of the senses.)

If I could grab each new writer by the shirt and yell an ironclad rule in their faces, it's this one. Whenever something new gets introduced to us, the readers, it should have some kind of description (assuming it's a tangible thing that *can* be described, of course). If it matters to the story then it deserves a description when it is first introduced. It really is that simple.

Your reader cannot see inside your mind. You might see your character as clear as day, but without writing down that image for us to read, we're left in the dark. More than once I've read through a rough draft trying to visualize a character, only to find out much later in the story that the writer had a completely different idea than the one I was forced to come up with on my own. Why didn't they just include that description when they first showed up?

Remember: All the senses are important. Each reader is going to have bias towards one or another—some use their ears more than the average person, some smell more, others feel the air with their skin. Leveling up your descriptive game includes all the senses, so long as they fit within the context of the story.

As a brain in a jar, your readers don't know what your chiseled-abs vampire lord who is as fearsome on the battlefield as in the bedroom actually *looks* like beyond his chiseled abs. I'm sure most of us might imagine someone handsome, but if you never show us what his face actually looks like (chin, lips, nose, eyes, you get it), then the reader is free to imagine this lusty blood-sucker as a total doofus. You can't rely on implication and suggestion alone, as there are more than a few readers who lack imagination, or worse—your readers might be complete weirdos.

It's best to approach this as a habit to develop. Try to be aware of when you bring in a new character or bring the story to a new location, and in that moment take as much time as you need to give your reader (aka your editor) the full, complete, detailed descriptions—far more than you think is necessary. **We're writing a rough draft, not the final product, so concepts and concerns about over describing do not apply here.** Go so far past wild that your descriptions become feral. The magic of editing and drafting will soothe this raging beast in time, so better to start off as strong, rich, and detailed as possible first.

In Summary

Descriptions can be your greatest storytelling device. One of the lines that separate good writers from great writers is how well they can incorporate their descriptions into the story itself.

A well-done description can do as much to advance the plot or character development as a dozen paragraphs just outright telling the reader stuff.

Let's get into that more, by way of characters and environments.

Characters

Your story's characters are more important than the story itself.

At least as far as rough drafts go, having strong, well-defined characters will make the drafting process vastly easier than working with characters that are weak or ill-defined. People like to praise good stories as being 'character-driven'—a term of endearment that simply means that the characters are so well-developed that their participation in the plot seems to be one of command, rather than the actual reality that all stories are only author-driven.

A unique and diverse cast of people is also important for the reader's ability to remember who is who. Your rough draft is a party, right? We all have some experience of going to a party and meeting a lot of new people all at once. **It can be difficult to remember a dozen new names**, let alone the relationship between all these new people. The more different you make your characters, the better chance your readers will have in remembering just who the hell these people are and why they matter.

Having well-developed characters can also provide easier solutions to plot-related structural issues. If your story is in a situation that you cannot think your way out of, return to the main character as a concept that exists independently of the plot. What *other* choices would this character make than the one you first thought of? Where is the conflict between their internal and external motivations that led to this difficult situation? Where would your character make a different choice than the one you set out for them?

A surprising number of potential story issues can be resolved not by addressing the plot, but simply by taking a closer look at the characters involved. So let's take a minute to go over some of the major considerations while developing your characters and letting them loose in your made-up world.

Fill in the Blanks

To the reader, a character is a set of descriptions, actions, and dialogue. Much like the story structure itself, a character is an outline that the reader has to use their imagination to fill in. The more we can define this outline, the more vivid your reader's imagination can get, and the better writer you'll appear to be.

Describing a character, then, is much more than simply stating facts about how they look; it's about conveying an entire being using details to imply the entirety of a person. The details you use to describe them should be pertinent to the story, or a physical allegory to their flaws/strengths. In other words, it's never *just* a type of smile—that character's smile speaks to the soul behind it, for better or worse.

And yeah, this is rough-draft stuff. Your characters may grow and evolve over not only the course of the story, but also over the course of drafting with your editor. Having a lot of traits to work with during that process is going to be better than having to constantly apply more traits as the story progresses.

If traits and mannerisms are added in later to 'flesh out' a story, the somewhat arbitrary nature of adding in details might accidentally lead to some conflicts between the characters, their choices, and the story itself. In other words, it might be better to start off with strong characters and adjust the story, than a strong story with ill-defined characters.

Introductions

Our first introduction to a character sets the reader's understanding of who this character is and sets expectations about who they'll be later. This is true in reading because it's true in real life. First impressions matter.

First Contact Context

The human brain uses associations to create memories. One trick to recalling information that you can't quite remember is to try and remember something you associate with that missing memory. Following the trail of association is how we remember people from our past, how we can recall old information, or otherwise jog our memories.

We could talk at length about how the context of a character's introduction dictates how the reader is going to feel about that make-believe person, but I believe this is somewhat self-evident. **How a character is introduced informs the reader who that character is in their basic essence.**

For example, if you introduce a character as they're working on a car, the reader will not only assume they're handy and know how to repair machines, but will also make a myriad of assumptions about that character based on the personality traits they associate with people in that profession.

This is just how humans work. Consider the instinctive human process that occurs when meeting someone new for the very first time. In real life, a stranger is assessed in the *context* of the meeting. Shaking hands with a stranger at a friend's chill party will significantly influence how you assess them, compared to meeting a stranger in a back alley late at night.

When you introduce a character, whoever your POV is should take into consideration the context of said meeting. What that context is will determine which qualities your POV will spot first. In a dangerous or action-heavy situation, assessing potential threats is going to be a priority. That means elements like body shape and size, what they're holding and wearing, their actions, words, and overall vibe are going to be spotted at a higher priority than, say, how nice their smile is, or what scent they're wearing (generally speaking, unless those elements are important later).

In a relaxed and safe situation, what your POV notices first will depend a lot more on who your POV is as a character. In a romance, attractiveness will be a high priority, with attention on clothes, hair, face, demeanor, and so on. Maybe they remind them of an ex-partner, maybe they've never seen someone like this before. In a detective novel, the protagonist may notice odd details normal people overlook. **How your POV assesses a new character by describing them to the reader tells us just as much about the POV as the character being described.**

In an omniscient third person, how a character is described is on the author themselves, so be aware that without a specific character point of view, how you talk about these make-believe people is a reflection of how you might feel about people like that yourself.

You're certainly free to switch it up—just as long as there's some rationale for doing so. There are some genres where a back-alley stranger might be initially assessed primarily in terms of their sexuality or attractiveness. Knowing your audience and genre expectations goes a long way in determining how your main character meets others.

Face and Clothing

Any character is naturally going to change over the course of a story. Not always, of course—some serialized series rely on their main character *not* changing. Or perhaps you have a god-like character whose unchanging nature is part of their story.

Those aside, most people are going to want to read about your characters and see their growth over the trials and tribulations of your story. Describing your characters is the easiest way to show this without outright telling your readers. And the easiest way to do that is to have a character start off looking one way, and then by the end have them look a completely different way.

If you do it right, we can see a character unravel before our eyes simply by talking about hairstyles and clothing. A well-groomed and polished noble can gradually lose that posh and polish over a stressful situation. If you did your introduction properly, we'll have the image of every hair in place. Then, as the story unfolds and the character is affected, one of those immaculate hairs is now *not* in place. A few buttons get missed. Smooth silken jackets get wrinkly. Dark circles start appearing on a youthful face.

Or, the reverse. A character who is introduced by describing the physical details of how they're a slob in rags, only to gradually show us this character as they grow and change, to arrive at someone who is now well put-together as their circumstances improve.

Lateral moves, too. Rather than going up or down in mental health as evidenced by their appearance, they can incorporate clothing, smells, or mannerisms as the story demands. A stranger in a strange land can gradually incorporate aspects of this new society into their words, demeanor, clothing, and actions.

We've all seen and read stories where the hero cuts off their long hair to show them getting over conflict or worry, or as a signal to the audience that the character is letting go of the past and focusing on what needs to be done. A good wardrobe change can show ten pages' worth of exposition in a single moment. The pampered royal youth donning street clothes or armor is always a pivotal moment in the story. You get the idea.

Clothing is also important from a world-building perspective. Pay close attention to what a character wears as a means of informing the reader where they're from. For example, a character from a colder climate might primarily wear spun wool or furs, while someone from a hot climate might wear silks or light cottons. In a fish out of water situation, a character might cling to their traditional garb despite the climate of their new location, making them miserable as they overheat/shiver and pushing their character growth by their need to adapt despite their desire to retain their original sense of self.

There's no limit to the way you can use character descriptions to tell a character's journey through your story. So, rather than *telling* your readers your character is a certain way, the question is: How can you *show* us this character trait through a description of how they look?

Body Types

One trap I often see new writers fall into is the 'everyone is hot' trope. I'm not opposed to hot characters, but when an entire story involves nothing but hot people (even the people on the street are knockout beauties), the story veers sharply into the uncomfortable and runs the risk of reading like lower quality writing.

The real world we actually live in is wildly variable, and when it comes to humans, we're all over the place. Presenting your readers with a wide variety of body types is an easy way for a fictional world to seem more vibrant and alive. And it's worth pointing out: everyone has a different definition of attractiveness. Even if you tried to make everyone in your story hot, there may be many readers out there who consider what you find sexy to be a big turn-off.

Since we're objectifying characters, think of them like a buffet table. If a buffet only offers one type of food, it's a disappointment - you could call it a *trough*, even if that one food is really good. A great *buffet* table offers all sorts of foods, so each visitor can fill up their plates with the snacks they personally find the tastiest.

Since this is a rough draft, we don't have to be overly worried about matching body types with personalities from the jump. Here are some quick examples of methods you might use to make sure you're presenting a diverse cast of characters.

- Body roulette: Use a random generator for different shapes, weights, heights, and the like, then spin that wheel for each character. Find creative ways to incorporate those traits when you introduce them.

- Replication: Watch a TV show or movie, and give your characters the same bodies of the actors therein. In other words, pick actors or celebrities as templates for your rough-draft characters to build on. You can even use celebrities or other real-life characters you dislike as the inspiration for your villains appearance and mannerisms.

- Bingo Card: Develop a list of diverse body types, and for each character, create a 'bingo' on the card. Simply trace out non-repeating patterns on that card to ensure all the options get used without too much overlap.

Trauma and Injuries

Injuries can vary between the extreme physical to the subtle emotional depending on your story and genre, but it's hard to have a compelling story without your main character being injured in some way.

These injuries can often be called 'flaws'—but I dislike the idea of flaws, as they imply the existence of a flawless character as an ideal. A flawless main character is probably a pretty boring one. If relatability is your aim, then rather than think of your characters as flawed, consider them *harmed* and in need of healing or relief.

How does your hero seek out this peace or relief? How does that contrast with your villain, who is seeking the same thing through different means? How do these characters use their pain while interacting with the external world? How does this pain influence how they treat themselves? And, if you're feeling up for it, how does this relate to yourself and what you're personally bringing to this story?

Injuring your main character is also a great method of showing the stakes of your plot. Stakes and injuries pair nicely together, like cheese and wine or some other overused metaphor like that. A character's scar (physical or emotional) can inform the reader of what happened when they failed once in the past, which can easily be leveraged to show how much worse it could be if they fail this time.

Also like stakes, character injuries are best when paired between external and internal. I suggest playing around with wounding your main characters in obvious and subtle ways. The pain that inspires one character to be a hero might be the same pain that causes another character to be a villain.

Old injuries are a fairly standard way to show your main character's past and the ghosts that haunt them. You have the option of having these old wounds ache whenever the thematically appropriate moment arises. They can be a source of shame, disgust, or even honor. They can be obvious and visual or internal and subtle.

A classic example of this is a grizzled character with an eyepatch. The mystery of how she lost her eye can be revealed during a vulnerable moment of reflection. The villain killed all her companions but spared her, taking her eye as "something to remember me by." A cruelty only a villain could think of, the missing eye isn't *just* a missing eye—it represents the character's failure to stop the bad guy and/or save the lives of her friends. The eye is both an external and internal injury. As such, her internal stake in the story becomes clear (revenge or similar), along with the external stakes (if the current characters don't stop the villain, they all might die too).

When you imagine your characters, try to develop the habit of imagining their injuries equal to their strengths. This is your rough draft, so refer back to these elements as often as you can—your editor will let you know when it's too much, a result much preferable to not having enough references and needing to add more later.

Accents and Mannerisms

Odd accents and strange mannerisms are a great way to give characters depth while broadening the world your story takes place in. If you're working in a fantasy or science fiction setting, you'll likely have a wide variety of magical places where the story doesn't take place—simply importing one or two characters from these lands will make your world appear vibrant and wide.

Moreover, these elements can be vitally important to certain genre tropes. In a mystery or thriller, small details can give the reader a hint of who might be lying or pretending to be someone they aren't. An accent can be a source of pride or a cause for prejudice. Mannerisms can show social class or rank, or hint at a character's true motivations or trustworthiness.

By now you've seen the trend and can probably guess what I'm going to suggest here: Go wild with it. **Type out your accents as they might sound if spoken.** If your main character can't understand someone due to their accent but the reader can, it makes them look either dumb or racist. If the reader can't understand what a side character is saying and neither can your MC, then that's reasonable, but what's even more fun is if the reader can't understand what a character says but your main character *can*. In that case we see a depth to your MC that tickles the imagination—why or how can they understand someone we can't?

Mannerisms are a shortcut to developing characters that are easier to remember. If you've got an ensemble cast, it can be hard for the reader to keep track of everyone. Having characters with strong and varied mannerisms can help the reader remember who is who.

The Myth of the Conscious Character

One common complaint among authors is that their characters seem to make choices that go against the established plot. To hear some say it, it's as if their characters are alive in the sense of being self-deterministic, and the hapless author is held hostage as they type out the character's whims.

On one hand, this is a fun way to think of your characters as strong and fleshed out. To know a character's personality and traits so intimately that you're writing primarily from what you believe they would naturally do is, in theory, a fantastic example of how to write a character-driven story.

However, sometimes I get the feeling that some authors truly believe this to be the case. I fear this veers into mental health territory, so let's be really clear about a few things.

Your characters are not real.

Your characters don't do anything and they make no choices.

You are in complete control of your story and characters.

Sock puppets, for example, are fun to make and horse around with. But believing your sock puppet is alive and conscious, that this sock is capable of making its own decisions and your hand

and mouth have no choice but to play along, takes something fun and moves it into an uncomfortable situation for others. If someone tries to tell you their sock puppet is *real* and it is the one choosing what to say, you'd rightly be worried about the person.

So, too, I worry about writers who genuinely believe their characters are real in some sense. If the writer doesn't believe they're in control of their story, or believes a conscious character deliberately changes the story to suit their needs, then the final product will suffer in quality.

A character-driven plot is still in need of an excellent plot. You, the author, are the final arbiter of the plot as well as the characters therein. If a character you've developed doesn't fit your story, create a new character who does, or create a new plot for that character to exist in.

Your editor doesn't believe your characters are real and will give you feedback with that in mind. Your readers won't believe they're actually real, either. Work towards the goal, and if some aspect of your story doesn't fit, like an unruly character, then get rid of it. It's that easy.

Locations

Like it or not, your environments and locations are as much 'characters' in your story as the people are. As such, your environments need as much attention as they do, as you can tell a great deal of your story through their description as well.

In fact, you can apply everything I wrote under Characters to how you approach describing your environments. But I'm trying to boost my word count here, so we're going to get into the details regardless.

Description Types

One of my biggest frustrations in editing is the lack of environmental descriptions. This is particularly frustrating in fantasy settings, but it persists no matter what genre is put in front of me. People who read fantasy, science fiction, and the like love to be transported to new and magical worlds. *Not* describing those worlds to your readers is a grave crime against not only the literary arts, but against the readers themselves, and I will testify against you in court.

Again: *if new, then describe.* In the same way that our human brains have automatic processes when meeting a person for the first time, we do the exact same thing when we arrive in a new location. In other words, we use all our senses to evaluate a location, with the context of that discovery dictating the priorities of what we see.

I divide environmental descriptions into three broad categories: Long Distance, Mid-Range, and Up Close. Paying attention to each one when appropriate to the story is vital to showing your readers your world at large. The better you do, the more your brain-jar readers will feel alive, almost like they're breathing the same air as your characters.

Long Distance

Long distance descriptions are simply the view a character sees from afar. One doesn't have to be up high to see far, although that always helps. A character entering into a new kingdom might see a meadow stretching off into some distant woods, or a long and potholed street that snakes deeper into an abandoned city. Distance can be arbitrary, but typically excludes smell, taste, and touch, in favor of sight and possibly sound.

This is worth digging into, as the lack of long-distance descriptions is one of the most common frustrations I see in rough drafts. This is wild to me, especially in fantasy and science fiction settings. You build an entire fantasy world. Why would you *not* show that to your readers?

As your editor, I want to see it all: The rough and dirty city that never sleeps and never forgives. The giant forests that lead into meadowed mountain valleys. The tall spires of an ancient city of magic, double suns glinting off the electro-metallic plating. The lands darkened by clouds and the hue of the wet soil that stretches to the hazy horizon.

The storytelling opportunities here are endless. Yes, storytelling. Part of your story is embedded in the landscape itself. As characters, your locations and landscapes can change as much as the people do, so by the same mechanism we can see the story progress simply by seeing how the descriptions of environments change over time.

Example: War

Wars, unlike a small battle or skirmish, are too large to be kept secret. They don't just come out of nowhere, no matter how upset your indignant noble might be when his betrothed runs off with the roguish prince from the neighboring kingdom. Wars take months to build up to at the very least, and that process is nearly impossible to hide.

Soldiers need to be recruited and trained. Often in fantasy, that means villages and towns are going to lose a lot of people as they leave for training. It means blacksmiths are busy working on armaments and armor. It means fletchers are making arrows by the hundreds. It means supplies on wagons being transported to and fro. Makeshift forts, security checkpoints, lookouts for spies and scouts.

Building up to a war leaves an impression on the land. Forests cut down for siege engines and fuel. Creeks are dammed up. Smoke where iron is being smelted. Pristine nature corrupted as its resources are extracted in the endless pursuit of people killing each other can transform a magical fantasy kingdom as much as any character can change over the course of a story.

The reverse is just as true. After a war, a land can heal, but might remain as scarred as any living thing. The story you're telling can be reflected in the landscape itself, adding in that extra element that English teachers love.

Mid-Range

I define 'mid-range' as anything close enough to see, hear, or smell, but maybe not touch or taste.

A classic example is a fantasy protagonist stepping out of the rain and into a small roadside inn. Playing up the contrast between two environments is an easy slam-dunk for descriptions. The warmth of the large hearth, the smell of stew and ale, the lamp lights, the huddled patrons—the more you bring to the reader, the more we step into the inn with that character.

This level of attention to detail *should* be universally applicable. Again, whenever your character or story transitions between one location and another, that is the time to describe the new location.

Fantasy example aside, this is true for any genre, even contemporary. Setting a story in our modern day doesn't give an author an excuse to get out of describing environments—if anything, the emphasis should be on describing them with more attention and detail, since we're not in a 'fantasy' and are thereby more restricted in our imaginations.

Example: Home

A hero's home is a great place to showcase how mid-range descriptions can impact the emotional resonance of a story. If you're writing a tale of lost innocence, a beautiful-yet-humble home can showcase the scents, sounds, and sights of a childhood as a touchstone for when innocence is lost later. The smell of a home-cooked stew with a specific herb or spice can bring the hero a truly emotional moment during their rock-bottom moment, as the sudden reminder of their home and who they used to be contrasts heavily against the emotional weight of the conflict.

For a character who grew up in a terrible home, the reverse can also work in any number of ways. A smell or sound can trigger the character into believing they never truly escaped that horrible place. Or perhaps it can alert the character to something rotten going on behind the scenes of a location or character that seems fine.

The point here is that describing a mid-range location, especially early in the story, can give the readers both a sensory and emotional anchor that the story can refer back to and build upon later.

Up Close

Anything close enough to touch or taste is 'up close.' As you can imagine, this is often rather intimate, violent, or investigative.

This is where a lot of non-visual senses can shine, especially smell, taste, and touch. Skin might be either soft or rough, but a person can *smell* any kind of way. Absolutely take the time to decide what all your main characters smell like, and if possible, give an in-world reason as to why. A lingering hint of a specific smell in a room can tip a character off to who was recently there, or any number of other situations where a slight whiff of a particular scent is enough to trigger an important plot moment.

Taste can obviously play a big role in spicier scenes, both literally and figuratively. Taste is often the most neglected sense in storytelling, but one trick to find moments to include it is as smell-adjacent. If there's an overpowering smell, a character usually ends up with the taste of it in their mouths.

Example: A Cup of Tea

A cup of tea can be so much more than a cup of tea. That hot leaf juice has an unlimited number of smells and tastes—not to mention color and even consistency. The method of preparation and how the tea is presented tells the reader a lot about the world and culture of your story.

Is it a strong brew made from local herbs and served in a wooden mug? How about a rare herb from distant lands, served in ornate crystal teacups? How about a standard tea bag that no one remembers buying, that's how old it is, but the main character is desperate enough to try it? What if the tea was actually coffee?

Matching Location with Story

This feels somewhat self-evident. Matching your landscape with the tone and plot of your story is a pretty standard thing to do. But as you may suspect at this point, I'm going to make some outlandish and impractical suggestions on how to go about considering your setting with the tone and pace of your story.

Is your story gritty and dark? You'd expect such a tale to take place in a similarly gritty and dark location. Yes, you can switch it up. A gritty and dark story in a bright and lovely location would certainly be a challenge. The reverse is also true—a bright and happy story in a gritty and dark location could also be a significant challenge. But despite the challenge, there is certainly no shortage of stories that attempt to do this very thing, to varying degrees of success.

I'm about to do something similar here. While this guide thus far has encouraged experimentation and wild abandon when it comes to your rough draft, **I do urge some caution when it comes to clashing story tone with setting** unless it cuts directly to the heart of the story you're trying to tell.

In other words, unless a large point of the story is showcased with the juxtaposition of story and location, deliberately mismatching location and story just to be different or unusual rarely works. Of course I still encourage experimentation, but within a degree of reason—the last thing I want to do is hand your draft back with the note that your location undercuts or robs your story of the emotional weight you might have been going for.

Ah, who am I kidding? Just do whatever you like! Your manuscript evaluator will let you know what they think, which can give you the insight you need to decide if your story needs a change of venue or not.

How to End a Rough Draft

A story's ending is as important as the beginning. However, I would argue that for an indie author not concerned with nailing that agent-friendly opening hook, a story's ending is actually *more* important than the beginning.

It's no surprise that literary agents only concern themselves with the beginning lines, since their only concern is *selling* books. And they're right—your beginning is one of the biggest factors in whether or not a potential reader will purchase a book. A strong start is absolutely vital for grabbing a reader's attention, not to mention for the story's own sake!

But what makes a story truly unforgettable isn't the beginning—it's how the story ends.

This is quite natural if you think about it. We know nothing and feel nothing at the start. We have no relationship with the main character. We don't know about the world, magic, or any other storytelling elements. A beginning has to wow us without us knowing anything.

An ending, however, can wow us at the moment when we know and feel the most about everything. The ending is where the reader is the most invested in what will happen to our characters. It follows, then, that an ending has the potential to be vastly more impactful than a beginning.

Consider this from the perspective of other forms of art, especially with TV shows and movies. We've all been in a situation where a friend has forced us to endure the beginning of a show or movie with the acknowledgement that "It takes a while to get started," or similar assurances. They assert that a level of trust is required, as once the story takes off, it really goes hard, and the ending is unlike anything you've seen before. Perhaps you have been that friend, desperate for someone to talk to about how mind-blowing it all was in the end.

As it is, one of the most common concerns a client brings to me is about their endings. And for good reason—the endings of rough drafts are often the weakest part of the manuscript. So let's dig into some common pitfalls and see how you can draft a killer ending into even the roughest of your rough drafts.

What Makes a Satisfying Ending?

Hell if I know. There's no true answer to this question, as a satisfying ending to your specific story relies on too many variables to be able to authoritatively conceptualize in a universally applicable guideline. **What makes a good ending depends on what your story is.** What follows is some of the generalized advice I give to clients during the drafting process regardless of their specific story.

Remember the Beginning

A freakishly common issue I notice during manuscript evaluations is what I call *beginning amnesia*. This condition arises when the start of the story begins in a particular location with particular side-characters, but by the end we've forgotten all about them.

Typically, a satisfying ending wraps itself up in a circle, recalling the beginning through the lens of character and plot development. This doesn't have to be the boring 'hero's journey' where the MC comes back home but 'changed.' Your MC is free to be wherever they want to be at the end. The reader, however, might enjoy remembering how it all got started.

Let's say your privileged MC is ready to begin their coming-of-age quest. They begin in their fancy estate with their haughty or unusually supportive parent(s), along with a handful of servants, trainers, childhood friends, and the like. Classic beginning fantasy setup, right? But by the time the MC saves the world and you wrap up that story, these beginning characters have been wholly forgotten.

Consider reviewing your opening chapters when it comes time to structure your ending. Who deserves to know the fate of the main character? Do we leave a parent concerned without even a letter to let them know what's happened? If you start off a story with someone caring for your main character, it seems almost cruel to not let the reader know what happened to them and their concerns.

The bigger point is that a story can be more satisfying to the reader by giving said reader clues and references to the beginning. This is so we can see how far we've come along with the MC when the story wraps up. We all went on this journey together. We touched the heights and struggled through the depths. Remembering how far we've come is a great way to give your readers a strong sense of accomplishment, possibly alongside a big boost of dopamine that realization brings.

How you bring in those early characters and moments is up to you, but remember that the end can summarize as much as it concludes and would be all the stronger for it.

Honor Your Heroes

We've been through hell and back. Your heroes gave everything they had to win the day. Indeed, they gave more of themselves than they even knew they were capable of at the start. Their sacrifices and hardships are so much more than the external—as readers, we know the internal strife and sacrifices they made as well.

Heroes are often relatable for their hardships and sacrifices. We all make sacrifices every day. We struggle and strain, we grapple with difficult issues and fight villains as much as any fictional character could. All too often, these personal struggles of ours go unnoticed or unappreciated by the wider world. To read a story in which a hero struggles mightily, only for that hero's actions and sacrifices to go unnoticed or unappreciated in their fictional world, is the very opposite of a satisfying ending. It's outright heartbreaking.

The easiest way to deliver a satisfying ending to practically any story is to have people celebrate and honor the hero's victory.

If your character saved the world, having someone formally and publicly thank and honor them is certainly one way to deliver a satisfying conclusion to your story. This plays into our own deeply held convictions that we, too, should be honored for our own heroics. We might not get that in life, but we can damn well sure get it in our stories and live vicariously through our heroes all the more.

Remember, the movie didn't end with the evil space station blowing up. It ended in a celebration, a medal ceremony honoring the heroes who saved the day. That final, tonic chord that punches down while everyone claps and cheers for the heroes is pure fantasy juice straight to the adrenals. That satisfaction comes not because your heroes saved the day—it happens because they're being *honored* for saving the day. That's a proper hero's reward. Your hero deserves it because we all deserve it.

Of course, endings don't have to be this bombastic. Depending on genre and storytype, a subtler and more understated acknowledgement can work just as well. One character's private thanks can be more than enough for a true hero. Whatever this looks like in your story and world will depend entirely on your story and world.

Just remember—**if a hero saves the day but no one notices, it's probably a sad ending**, even if you try to sell the reader that being acknowledged doesn't matter. The concept goes against our most basic, instinctive need to be recognized by our tribe for our contributions, so that we ourselves feel like we matter.

By the same token, if you want a sad ending that leaves your readers haunted, having the world and people ignore your hero's sacrifice is the easiest way to get there. Anything presented here can be reversed if the ending you have in mind is deliberately bittersweet, sad, or anything else. It may end up just as good, as there are many tastes and preferences, and a strong sad story can be just as satisfying as any other.

Writing for a Stand-Alone

Begin with the end in mind.
Isn't it interesting how so many books and movies never seem to end on a final "the end" anymore? This 'Hollywood Never-End' trope makes a lot of sense when you think of your art as less an art and more of a test subject for market trends. Everyone wants a universe of unending interconnected stories, stories that only end when enough people lose interest.

While this "never say 'the end'" makes developing sequels much easier, it also robs the audience of a true sense of satisfaction. Applied across the movie industry for the past few decades, it's no wonder that everyone has ended up sick of endless sequels, prequels, and spin-offs. When no story ever truly ends, stories begin to feel like empty calories—always more, but never narratively filling.

Fortunately, as an indie author, you're about as removed from Hollywood considerations as anyone can be. This means you're free to deliver a stunning 'The End' with such force and power that a hundred movie executives will crap their pants without knowing why.

If your intention is to write a single, self-contained story, then **you have no excuse for having a weak ending.** In other words, if you know the story does not extend past the last page, then you have every reason to make that last page the most impactful moment anyone has ever read.

Again, what this looks like for your story is something only you alone can truly know. But in terms of outlook and attitude,

I suggest thinking about your ending with the same level of attention and passion as your beginning. That means thinking about your ending throughout the drafting process, not just when you get near your target word count and start to wonder how you're going to wrap all of this up.

You can still write a sequel even if you completely end a story. In fact, I'd argue a sequel pulled whole-cloth from inspiration would be a more fun read than a sequel long-planned that did not get the chance to grow with the author over time. How many unnecessary stories have been slopped out to readers, not from a sense of excitement, but rather than simply fulfilling a long-held contractual obligation? Ending a story completely means that any new entries to the now-series would come from a place of excitement and inspiration, not obligation.

And besides, this is just a *rough* draft. Tinkering with how open or closed to leave the ending is part of the drafting process.

Writing for a Series

I love ambition in writing, and going for a series straight out of the gate is a great way to learn a lot of hard lessons at the start of your career. I've said it a dozen times by now: I'm not here to tell you how to write your stories. That said, there is a mindset when it comes to writing a series that needs close examination before deciding how your plots play out.

There is a 'trap' of sorts that series-writers can fall into, and that's thinking of your series as just one really, really long story broken up into 'books' rather than by narrative structure. This is the easiest way to have a disappointing ending. So how do we avoid this outcome?

A good series is most likely going to have more than one plot line. The series in our hypothetical example could have, let's say, one major plotline per book in the series. A trilogy, then, would have three major plotlines that weave their way through the story.

Telling three concurrent stories means all three are only at the end of their Act 1 by the end of the book, which can end up feeling like a waste of time, or like the story isn't going anywhere. It is difficult to get readers excited about the second book in your story if your first book's ending falls flat. They'll not only be disappointed by the lack of narrative payout for all the reading, but they'll get the idea that your next book, or the series as a whole, might also be similarly disappointing.

The trick to ending the first book in a series is **still to deliver a satisfying ending to the primary plot**. But as the series has *three* plots that are equally important to the full tale, this seems an impossible task. *Which one is the 'primary' plot?*

So herein lies the suggestion: Assign one primary plot to each book, and let the other two plotlines take a step back from the story. This is an potentially excruciating idea for someone who has their sights set high, but fortunately we're only working on the rough draft right now. You have room to experiment.

If you've written all three plots out equally, try cutting and pasting most of two of those plotlines into their own document. In fact, having three equally developed plotlines allows for easy cutting and pasting to see which one shines the most for your first book, which might make the best primary for the second, and so on. Cutting and pasting can leave your original draft intact, making these experiments risk-free.

Using another food analogy, there's a reason people enjoy eating slices of pizza over picking up the entire thing and trying to eat it as a whole. Our minds and our mouths can only open so wide. It's much more fun to insert something that fits, rather than shoving in something too large. You have a grand story to tell, that's fine. Don't shove it all in your reader's face at once. Pick a primary plot for each book and we can eat it just fine.

Since a series not only has to deliver a great story, it also has to convince your readers that the final ending is going to be even more amazing than your first book's ending. And the only way to do that, that I know of, is to nail that first plot's ending with the same passion and deliberate effort as a stand-alone.

The only difference between writing a stand-alone and a series is that, after you've knocked your reader's socks off with that stellar ending, you pull the "... meanwhile, this side plot point is now getting to be more important ..." hint that will leave your readers drooling for the next installment.

Write the Last Chapter First

We're engaging in suggestions, not commands, but I want to make the case for trying this method if it comes easily to you.

It certainly helped me. When I first started writing after a long absence, I knew from the onset that I wanted to publish novels. After repressing my creative side for more than a decade, the ideas for these novels came at me like a burst dam. I knew I had to set up some rules for myself or risk getting washed away, in the sense that I would be cursed to forever chase new ideas while leaving the old ones behind. To cut through that stream of creativity, I decided that I would not start writing a story unless I knew exactly how it ended.

This is where inspiration comes in. I don't know how to think up an ending to a story when I don't even know what the story is about. That sounds crazy. But inspiration—that moment of being inspired—is magical. The first thing I ever 'saw' in my own series is the last chapter. It came to me unbidden. I didn't know who the character I was seeing in my mind was, I didn't know what they had been through, I only knew what was happening here at the end of all those journeys. I went home, wrote it down, and that's how I started writing my series.

Since then, the last chapter of the last book has been a beacon across the dark and choppy waters of creativity. It has been the pure snow-capped peak as I thrash my way through the tangled-plot jungles to reach it. I have no anxiety about how this sprawling epic will end. In fact, I'm excited to get there. The destination is set, and the only question remaining is: What is the *coolest* way to get there?

It's quite fashionable to look down on inspiration. The War of Art and other motivational works disregard inspiration in favor of plain old hard work. While there is value in consistency regardless of feelings, I believe that any story that doesn't start off with that spark of true inspiration isn't worth reading or writing.

By "start off with" I don't necessarily mean "start" as in the beginning of the story. Inspiration for a story can come anywhere along the tale. However, with some focus and attention, cultivating the habit of thinking about a cool ending can be extremely helpful.

Knowing where you're headed can make the difference between frustration and completion. In terms of efficiency, given that you already know how the story ends, you can build in all the story beats as you go, rather than going back and changing the story to fit your ending later.

Again, there's no way to outline an ending, and there's no way to pants it either. Starting with the ending almost always requires creative inspiration. A story is defined by its beginning and its ending. Ideally, the two would work together, and a rough draft is a great place to experiment with connecting these ideas together.

The End is Dessert

Much like a dessert might be picked in concert with the meal beforehand, the actual specifics of how to end your story are going to be entirely dependent on the story itself.

Imagine a full course gourmet meal made for you by your personal chef (who is also you), where every dish is thought out not just in terms of quality but also in how the various tastes interact throughout the meal.

Then imagine the final dish—a dessert that *should* expertly put a bow on the culinary experience—is half of a stale store-bought cookie and a note that says "the *next* meal is going to be even better!"

In other words, a weak or disappointing ending can ruin the entire meal, or story. Reading, no matter how delightful it may be, is still an *effort*. People like to be rewarded for their efforts. **In storytelling, the best reward we can give a reader is a kick-ass ending.** Many wonderful stories have fallen into disrepute for ending poorly, so I believe working with your ending in mind is vital for a healthy, cohesive story.

But more importantly than impressing your reader, remember who your true and only real audience is: yourself. You're writing this decadent experience to imagine and savor a particular gourmet richness in a story that you just can't seem to get anywhere else. Instead of writing what you think might entice a reader for your next story, aim to give yourself an ending in your story so incredible that it makes you forget that you wrote it yousef.

Getting Over Writer's Block

Writer's Block is a lot like hiccups. Everyone has a remedy they swear by, each more convoluted and ridiculous than the last.

In my estimation, there are different types of writer's block. Here are my suggestions on how to approach them.

Not Knowing What to Write

Find inspiration. Don't wait around for inspiration to find you. Actively engage in other forms of art. Engage with yourself and who you are at this moment. Read, listen, watch, feel, taste, smell. Binge a cool show. Go for a walk. Find a new musical genre to obsess over.

Art in all forms inspires art of all forms. If you don't know what to write, seek out art, and find inspiration. What inspires you the most?

Knowing What to Write, but Not Writing It

A writer might find themselves knowing exactly what to write next, but for some reason, there is resistance to actually writing it down. The logical flow of the story, beat after beat, and all you have to do is write down the next beat—but for some reason you're dragging your feet.

This is a clear sign that you need to do something different. If you're not excited to tell this part of the story, why would anyone be excited to read it? A story written under obligation isn't a fun selling point, and betrays the entire point of this guide.

The easiest solution to this block is to come up with a better way to accomplish this part of the story. Is it the time to add a little unexpected revelation or action? Perhaps the scene would be better summarized in a line later, and can just be cut.

Whatever it is, the solution lies in a willingness to abandon the plan and go off-book. We're rough-drafting here, don't just give into logical story progression. If you don't want to write this section, think of a more fun section and write that instead.

Life Stuff

Sometimes 'writer's block' is just being tired. It can be burnout, lack of sleep, or illness. Taking a break can fix writer's block as much as anything else. Writing to the detriment of health isn't a sustainable writing solution—it can only lead to burnout and frustration.

Or maybe the spirit of inspiration has simply left, and now you've lost interest in the project. Writing novels is pretty low stakes in the context of the greater world, and writing a rough draft even more so. Abandoning a rough draft isn't the worst thing in the world. It may, in fact, be a fantastic choice, especially if it's done to chase a much better story idea.

Of course I would caution writers against abandoning their work too quickly. It is far too easy to get trapped in a loop of having a good idea > writing some of it > it turns into work > dropping it for a shiny new idea. Writing a novel is hard work, no matter how excited you are for the story.

But, as this is fundamentally an art, you're welcome to engage with it however you please. If writing half a rough draft, only to drop it to start a new one, is something you enjoy doing as your hobby, then I can't fathom any objections to it. Chasing new story ideas all the time will preclude actually finishing any of them, but that's your business. And since your art is your business, how you approach this is up to you.

Other Resources

I wanted to touch on other resources that have been used by writers to help with their rough drafts. Also, because this is my guide for potential clients, I've included my assessment of them.

Save the Cat Writes a Novel

Save the Cat Writes a novel is a touchstone how-to guide for beginning authors. Hardly a day goes by that a author-aspiriant finds this book and digs into it.

And for good reason: it's a coloring book.

Despite how that might read, I don't have any issues with it. In fact, for a beginning artist, a coloring book can be a fantastic way to work on skills like coloring, shading, cross hatching, and so on. The only thing a coloring book can't teach you is how to draw your own shapes, or more literally, it can't teach you how to draw your own pictures.

There are plenty of authors who have used Save the Cat as a template, coloring in the shapes with their own unique coloring schemes. There are plenty of people who enjoy these kinds of color-by-number books as well. As long as both writer and reader are enjoying themselves, I see no harm in it.

I have two suggestions on why you might want to not use Save the Cat while writing your rough draft.

Origin

Save the Cat originally started as a guide on writing screenplays. That book was wildly successful for a reason: it was specific to the industry. I have no doubt the original Save the Cat is a fantastic resource for writing movie and TV show scripts.

A novel is not a TV show. This seems fairly obvious, but less than I would have thought. The way you tell a story in a visual medium like TV is going to be vastly different than how you tell a story through the written word. It's like a guide to painting gets repackaged as a guide to carving marble sculptures—while there may be some superficial similarities between the mediums, the act of creation, and the means of appreciating the final result, are too dissimilar to be of any real help.

Boring

I'll just say it: The Save the Cat format is boring. Following the format doesn't ensure anything other than you followed the most basic formulaic story structure. If I already know the outline of your story by the first page, why would I be excited to see what happens?

Writing an excellent story with engaging prose about interesting characters in amazing locations has absolutely nothing to do with the narrative structure. By that I mean, any type of narrative structure works if it works with the story. I get a bit sad thinking about all the interesting and original stories that lost their originality because a beginning writer believed they needed to follow the coloring book's outlines rather than drawing their own pictures.

AI

The subject of AI and the introduction of services like ChatGPT dominate a lot of online discourse, so it's worth mentioning here. Personally, I'm anti-AI, anti-ChatGPT when it comes to creating art. I also don't work with clients who use it in their stories.

To me, the subject comes down to one question: **Do you want to write your story**, or do you want someone else to write it for you?

This may seem like a loaded question, but in all fairness, it's not. Ghostwriters have existed since the earliest days of literature. The publishing industry is widely known to hire as many ghostwriters as needed, especially for memoirs of celebrities who have neither time nor skill to write their books themselves.

Think about it like a painter who uses AI to create an image. The painter now has an image that approximates roughly what they might have had in mind. The result isn't the image—the result is that the painter doesn't have to paint. The result is a musician doesn't have to make music. A writer doesn't have to write.

For non-artists, this might seem like a wonderful thing. For an artist, this may not. I started writing because I loved the art of writing. Automating writing doesn't help me—it steals from me my favorite part of it all.

If you do not want to *write* your own story, why are you 'writing' a story?

Possible AI Uses

There may be some uses for it outside of generating prose. Much like an advanced Magic 8 Ball, asking questions about whatever difficulty you're having in outlining your story might yield some insights on how to overcome that challenge.

Of course, you can do the same with a pack of Tarot cards, talking to a friend or partner, throwing darts, spinning a wheel, or any other randomized option that can provide an alternative point of view to your story.

AI Limits

We are rapidly advancing to a world of the ultimate custom novel that can be generated by a layperson. Imagine a website where you type in your name, select your favorite genres and tropes, and a few moments later you're reading a novel custom-generated to your preferences with you as the main character. Another button press and that work could be printed with its own AI cover and on your doorstep mere days later.

With this reality looming on the horizon, it begs all sorts of questions that anyone tempted to use GPT should ask themselves. Chief among those questions should be: Why should anyone read *your* AI story when they can use that same AI to make their own just as easily, and more to their own preferences?

After all, if it's that easy to use for you, it's that easy to use for anyone else. That's why there is no inherent value in AI-generated anything—it is effortless to use.

The inherent value of a human-written novel is in the effort it took to tell it. The blood, sweat, and tears of the author is the foundation of value and meaning presented to the reader. Real human passion, drive, and dedication goes into writing. Those are the elements that a reader picks up on. We're all around the campfire telling each other stories. Having a robot replicate the form of a story around a campfire is the premise of a horror story, not an exciting future of self-expression.

There will never be a machine that can fully replace human-made art. Machines aren't capable of conceptualizing. Without the ability to understand an abstract concept, all any AI can be is a pattern-matching algorithm capable of mimicking human output. That's why AI, no matter how advanced it gets, will always appear a bit off, a bit creepy, a bit not right in ways that don't make sense.

AI doesn't understand what a "window" is, which is why a generated image of a window might have its frames fade or blend into the furniture. An AI writing a story doesn't understand that it's writing a story, and as such, the story itself will read oddly in discomforting ways that are hard to understand. Without the ability to understand abstract concepts, that will always be the inevitable result.

Technicality aside, the main point remains the same. I'm assuming that you've gotten into writing novels because you love writing novels. I'm assuming that the challenges that come your way will make you feel incredible when you find your way through them. And I'm assuming you want that immense, life-changing feeling of holding your first book in your hands to be free from the taint of cheating and shortcuts.

Don't rob yourself of the satisfaction you can take in your potential achievements. Don't use AI to write your books.

In Summary

If this guide wasn't helpful, I hope it was at least entertaining to read. I wrote it in six days, so this could be considered a bit of a rough draft itself. If it takes off, I will definitely return with a more thorough and well-researched second edition.

If we could read the rough drafts of our favorite novels, we might be shocked to find what seemed like a story beat carved by the gods might have been a last-second thought scribbled in the margins.

The primary goal of this guide is less about academic rigidity in story form and type, and more about providing inspiration to the writer. It is a cheerleader of sorts, built not as 'a guide to writing a story' but as a discussion of 'rough drafts, their goals, and what makes writing one harder than it needs to be.' I aimed to show that in this guide's rough structure and prose. It's not bad writing if it's deliberately that way, right? ...right?

There are no lower stakes than the rough draft of a novel. The primordial clay we pull from inspiration can take any shape while it is fresh and wet. We have all the time and resources we need to turn a rough draft into a final product.

Go forth, my writers, and enjoy creating your art.

Oh, and if you're looking for a manuscript evaluation, developmental edit, or beta read, check it out:

HyperNostalgia.org

Manuscript Evaluation Services

You can also email me at **rsk.author@gmail.com** - I hope to hear from you!

Acknowledgements

If there's anyone responsible for this guide being somewhat readable and semi-coherent, it's Megan G. Mossgrove. She took on this project like a champion and combed out all the rough bits to let my own brand of crazy shine through. If you want to hire Megan for editing, check out:

Megan G. Mossgrove

Mossgrovewrites.com - Mossgrovewrites@gmail.com

A big Thank You for Cara Blaine for formatting!

cblaine.com/services – admin@cblaine.com

I have to thank my online writing friends, from BookTok to IndieAuthorTok, to everyone in the writer-support discord servers. Your support and encouragement was the reason I had the confidence to become a freelance developmental editor, which directly led to this guide.

My Patrons from Patreon deserve a shout-out. The following people have gone above and beyond in supporting me. Please check out their websites:

Scott Roche - **scottroche.com**

Sam Washington - **spwashi.com**

Phyllis Khare - **PhyllisKhare.com**

If you want to be mentioned in my next novel, please consider supporting me on Patreon. All Patrons get a free eBook of my books, plus exclusive content, access to the discord server, and more!

Patreon.com/RSKrules

Buy me a coffee at Ko-Fi: **ko-fi.com/rskrules**

Finally, an enormous THANK YOU to my family, especially my mom. Your continued support has helped me build this foundation. It's all up from here.